Sparkling Droplets

POEMS

Written By

- Savita S. Dharan -

Publishers

Arclines Literary Club

Email: arclinesliterary@gmail.com

VIRAR- MAHARASHTRA-INDIA-401303

ISBN : 978-93-342-6660-3

POEMS

*****

1. The Rising Sun

Glaring from beyond the green bushy hills
Begins the solemn, ravish routine drills
The spread out of bright hue red orange ball
Brushed up all along horizon, giving wake-up call
Nature's lovely father sharing power
Light up with pride from high tower
Every morning, as steady as ever,
No flu-fever, tiring never.

Inspire all on earth to strive
For life's challenges, bold routine drives.
Splashing out illumine light
From behind the green mount's soaring height
Perfect timing with schedule tight

Ever ready reckoner, soldier's might
Steady movements forward sight,
Sparkle in splendid uniform white.

To dispel dark dozing eyes
All pious religious pay respects
Praying obligation,
Pouring holy water to hail,
As perked up pious minds wail,
To vanquish dreadful bad fungus, virus,
After the sordid heavy, stormy rains.

Banish all the sinners' sins
With thy hot blaze heat beams
Noon strides suck off fatty creams
The daily slogging masses dreams.
All living beings' source of energy
Cherishing generous rays.

Oh! Blessed blissful, prophet or clergy
Deep reverence, the grace souls' parody
Disbursing the moody slur-blur,

Evening shady malady prevail
Gleaming welcome prowl trail
Shiny still setting though,
Colorful sky pleasant glow
Viewers on beach bid goodbye row
Couples, Lovers bewitched bow,
Prime promise, faithful vow.
As the farmers mow, ply & plough
Your bounty rays energize crops heap grow
Veggies, fruits, flowers far wide scatter
Blooming beauty behold world, potent potter.

*****

2. College

Tense & nervous, as are school girls,
Enter college, more like young birds.
Learn to fly, for a heavy price,
With great aspects encouraged by parents.
Friends are made for names' sake,
Real ones been left in school.
New subjects, who's interested,
Master-keys, & guides can be purchased.
In the meantime, let's enjoy life,
Keep an eye on latest Filmfare, movie jive.
When lectures start, students fret,
All chat & laugh, without any thought,
Of their minds beginning to wrought.
Beware, dare exams are nearby,
If failure mars, crock tears may defy.
Then you'll have to hear scolds, shouts,

Pastings, puddings on head mounts.
Level-headed, comprise the mind,
Life ups-downs binds.
Never-mind, try & try on the whole,
You'll surely succeed in your goal.

*****

3. Newspaper

Black on white, I am bright
Read by all loose or tight
About me, people are crazy
But you know, I am not lazy
Here & there, anywhere
I am present everywhere.
People buy me for a price,
I am daily on the rise
It's for them, I care admire
They have not allowed me to expire.
I am a pleasure in their leisure
Since I provide them info
Of social, political friends or foe.
I carry news on my back
Fresh, old, bold, but not fake.
To let the people know reality

I serve people sincerely
Perform my duties honestly.
But I am afraid, the present state
Of this world has become full of hate.
Cheatings, corruptions, crimes,
Are prime features of this times.
Cases of robbery, dacoity & rioting
on communal ground are horrifying
Behaviors of human beings mainly,
Changing to crazy animals daily.
I know you all would like to disagree
But before that, read of the espionage
in our country.
I wish they make a special case study,
make the culprits pay for disloyalty,
I am ashamed to disclose anything anymore,
the frightful scenes of facts so sour,
But, beware the new rage age,
Of which I must not be in cage.
I wish someone, breaks the seal,
To give me a better life, at my will.

*****

4. My Brother

I often write letter, with some jitter
To my abroad working loving brother
Who loves us the most,
& serves well his post.

He dares to take,
Any task, not fake
To fulfil the demands
Of the family wants.

One of everlasting light,
He pulls us ahead of nightmarish nights.
I hope & pray, God's blessing rays,
May fall on him abundantly,
To make him healthy,

Progress to prosper
Without any regrets spur.
Ah! how glad every sister be
To have a brother like him,
As is me.

*****

5. Humanity

Human beings came into being
For the purpose of humanity.
Human beings live in this world,
With a cause for humanity.
Human beings stress on the point,
Of being humble for humanity.
Human beings pray,
To survive in humanity
Human beings fatefully do not possess,
Forever this invaluable jewel of humanity.

*****

6. Sea-Ways

I do not know the reason why?
Always strong waves of the sea cry.
The flow of water rises then ebb,
Showing its strength, whatever to grab.
The gentle feel of the breeze,
Wading wanderers cool, freeze.
The waves are drifting To - FRO,
Upon which I would swing & go.
Some make mounds on the shore,
Scribble off names of friends or foe.

The waves reach such distances,
To wipe them off & roar in distress.
Beneath, the mysteries frankly wide open,
Which aren't prankish, but of high value
token.

Under the rippling surfaces,
Lies varied species of many races.
Gorgeous wonders under the sea-bed,
Gives a taste of heavenly dreamland.
Oils, Oysters, Ember-Diamonds profound,
Keeps all eyes very well spellbound.

*****

7. Nature

A bounty pond, trees around,
Chirping birds flying, cheering valley-villas
abound.
Dawn break, orange ball emerges mid-
mount,
Dark blue gloom disarrays,
As the sun rises above in sky to jaunt.
Every day-break cycle deal,
Marvelous ruby red jewel none can steal.
Splendid profound solar light,
Infinite sparkle, Invaluable delight.

Village pathways sizzle dazzle,
Hilly trees, herbs, shrubs & herds whine,
Ample dabble of golden rays angelic divine.
Evenly rendered, treasure brim fine.

Common masses welcome the bright light,
Dusting off to clean the surround sight.
Homely dames' dry clothes,
Spread fragrant breeze,
Pious priests light incense sticks,
Take holy dips, water the plants, pay
obeisance.

Burning fireball energize above sky blur
Youth indulge in their burble core.
Elders deal in mid-day meal,
Medics predict quick heal,
Children play bare & dare outdoor,
While the parents snooze & snore.

Sportsmen perspire as they raid,
Small crowd cheer them in the shade.
Merry makers relieve, break ice,
Varied healthy drinks suffice.
Coy couples cluster on crags,
Evening clouds shelter the brags.

After the glorious global run,
Bidding adieu sets the sun.
Wagers, farmers return back home,
Comely ladies welcome, refresh their chums.

*****

8. Aloe-Vera

Alone and Aloof, frivolity fritter grove,
Beguile by destiny's grisly plight throw
Willy-Nilly Wilson waif Willow
Cozy ween gaze, out from the Pillow.

Thirsty as I lay, Thorn-thrust,
Desolate in the wild Worldly spurt.
You grip me to thrive on threshold
Flourished through thick and thin aboard.

To save my throne forgone, forlorn,
With firm grim, growl, groan,
Confined in the corner colossal charm
Although ripped off, all along
Chaste, chastity balm.

Fierce guts rebuild, Vigour sharp guise palm
Weather ravaged razed, though reaped your realm
Flowering out rebel revival, recompose, claim calm
Striving stunt subdue, subsist, sublime.
Onus age's gear berg chord,
Coy damsel's beauty guard.

Herbal remedy, skin ailments' blow
Marvel darts in meadow rows.
Oh! Aloe-Vera through centuries
May your grace gleam glow.

*****

9. Birds

Oh! how glorious birds God has made,
Sparrows, Crows, Mynahs appease
Wandering Doves for peace,
Bulbul pairs always at ease,
Parrots green with red neck-band,
True blue peacocks grace the garden land.
Eagles, Owls, Bats strain
though good-bad omen dogma domain,
Still Melody of Cuckoo's, Nightingales sing
sane,
Breaking the dawn's silent slur,
Marvelous color sooth minds, as sleepy eyes
blur.
Very few bite-bits do they eat,
Kingfisher, Seagulls swoon to fish,
Eagles, Vultures feat on meat

Keep their bodies ever fighting fit to fleet.

Birds of same feather, flock together,

Caring, sharing, bearing every weather.

Flocks of birds are flying high,

Wishing cheerful morning sky,

To one & all brave or coy.

Chirping on the trees,

Searching food in the grasses & fields,

Some birds bathing in puddles, ponds,

Enjoying fresh Sun's rays abound,

Fuzzing, Whizzing releasing breezy waves,

Pairing, daring river's ripple dodge agaves.

Small skillful plight to gather,

Straws, twigs to build perfect hidden nests yonder,

That modern architects would ponder.

As Eve sets, V-shaped swans' flight brave,

The skies limitless horizon jive rave.

Gentle gleam, punctual seam,

Magical magnificent beam.

We can just try to dream.

*****

10. Sunflower fields

Sparkling bright yellow star
Enhancing Sunny Shiny jour
Paying obeisance to sun rays near and far.
Aligned scatter agnate, Agile track
In the wild fields, attune attract back.
As bugle buoyant pioneer
Trail blazer blossom sheaf sheer
promote propel Peerless peer.
Waving pennant through breezy ruffle,
Shuffle salubrious,
salutary salute salvation pious.

*****

11. Rose Garden

If somebody try suppose,
To suggest, advice or propose
Than why not we try to compose?
A sonnet of this life morose.

Can't we fix up the leaking hose,
If nobody opposes, deposes, reposes
To grow a garden full of colorful roses.
Impact, impale impart, imbue,
Roses are red, violets are blue.

Heap, haul the fresh spring soil dew.
All eyes could glare, gleam, glue,
At the myriad marvel sight cue, due
Symbol of power, passion, energetic hue
Every red-letter day race,

Redeem, redress, refer, praise,
Consorts, Lovers, Teachers, Leaders hail,
Everybody's courtesy status portal hale.
Sharp zigzag edges of leaf & thorns green,
Brawl trespass of flies to vie away clean.

*****

12. Jasmine Virtue

White small lilies, Is it right?
Nay that's Immortal Jasmine bright.
Embed embellish to every sight
Emerge, emote, evoke, exam
Diminutive dignity dike dam
When dainty Jasmine dahlia dawdle past
Shy bride's tie bonafide bond
Build guild to bridge family ties all around
Gilt, gild with guts gusto profound.
Head covered garlands enhance her hairs
harmonize, heal heed heaving heiress.
Hierarchy highlight its majestic mount,
High-spirited hilarious heroine jaunt.
Oh! Jasmine's olfaction sense
Offer highly gifted tranquil trance.

*****

13. Lily lotus galore

Lots of us paying aegis grace
In bedazzle beatific moonlit rays.
Throughout ponds and lakes
Frolic furor, frugal, frost
White, pink, purple gaiety slot
Glorify calm, soothing moonlit night
Heal, Hail, heath, heave nature's plight
Open wide generous opulent petal all sides,
Perpend, perpetual peristyles blends.
Flawless Flank, flora flaunt all around.
Forbearance foster fragrance all abound.

*****

14. Marigold

Nature's vast love is true
Dahila of Orange, Maroon, Yellow
fit on green girdles, refresh meadow.
Beautiful flowers bloom, saplings sag
Enhancing fragrance, lustre gag.
Cheering, graceful Marigold
juts out of ramp, behold bold!
Recreate symbol of Symphony,
In temples, functions many.
Holy homage to all ages
Enshrined dieties; In prayer book pages.
Trance devotees' tranquil delight
Offered for rituals, solemnify noble plight.
Its status quo on every station
Diwali, Dusshera Celebration.
Precious, prestige jubilant celestial,

Part and Parcel of all Govinda, Ganesh
festival.
Topsy, Turvy hanging motifs mound,
Artful colorful designs on ground.
New Inauguration all around,
guards entrance at home abound.

*****

15. Aspire, perspire, don't despair

Horizon is my destination,
Goal is depth of the sea.
To conquer it- my aspiration,
Only then I will be free.

Mounts, valleys distort my way
Desserts, Oceans & Storms, although
I must succeed, come what may
Before its time to fall.

I see a bird soaring high
A wave of urge rushes through me
One day, even I shall fly.
Below, the world shall see,

When my aim is fulfilled, they will all agree.

With each & every step, my goal gets farther still,

Will I ever succeed?

But my heart is filled with hope & will

What more do I need?

*****

16. The Mango Trees

Special scent of the flowers blossom
In wide spread shade grove boom
As carefree breeze gush gusto bloom
Refreshing sweet grandeur loom.
Dense tall slender hallow leaves abound
Small sprouts of fruit hammocks
Hale, hail all around
Nutty, hard though for hey-day hiatus
Sun kissed mango trees', open apparatus.
Grasping all the environs' envy
Green serene stable prime privy
Raw everlasting sour savory.
Long days heat saga sabotage bearing,
Rigor rim rind ridicule rivalry sharing.

Rook roost rolls romance,
Prone, promote prompt chance.
Roots underneath of great virtue,
Grip rouse sheath vive undue
Setting sham service session,
Arouse romp roseate reflection.
As the fruit grows in full shape,
Shedding its raw sour in avid awe,
Agonize agony ail aim
Amigo, amity amorous, marvel claim.
Veracious venture vaunt veer,
Variant upheaval uplift vent virtues
Evince, evoke, evolve, exalt to choose.
"Ask for a boon to fulfill your wish",
"Grant me the sweetest flavor everyone could relish".
Gorgeous gracious Venus approve,
Glorify glamour glee glance move.
Prim pretty pristine cove coup,
Dominant pleasing doyen in fruits world troop.

*****

17. Indian Calendar Months

January: New year resolutions, desires, wishes, obligations. Republic day function. Marvel marshals' parade stout, stalk status.'Makar Sankranti', kite flying aspirations.

February: Favorite valentine partner's selection, for valentine day celebration.

March: Women's day glory, dates, rates, Selfie - photos. Holi- colourful mayhem. All Religious Celebrations, New dress wears, henna Designs.

April: Fresh crops, flowers, fruits, Nature's Invaluable gifts bonus. States enjoy, New Year festivals celebrations, flowers' decorations. Delicious dishes foods preparations.

May: Summer's mature saturation. Worker's day function, Site seeing pleasure excursion.

June: Praying for relief from heat, First rainfall

predictions, Schools and Colleges re-opening, Fresh young faces blooming, Onset of Indian monsoon, Refreshing breeze, wet mud's scent, Spreads warm welcome invitations.

July: Ashadi Ekadashi pious fasts, Muharram penance lasts.

August: Penance panacea, mass obeisance, 'Shravan', Holy month of Hindus solace fusion. Independence- day pompous fete, Festivals begin with Raksha Bandhan. 'Janmashtami','Onam', 'Ganpati' sweet delicacies, Sadya feast.

September: Eventual evolution, 'Teacher's day' exalt dynamic solution.

October: Birth anniversary of 'Father of Nation'- Mahatma Gandhi, Of 'Jai Jawan Jai Kisan'- Former PM. Lal Bahadur Shastri, great veteran leaders, freedom Fighters memories, due respects paid in Stern reverence. 'Navratri festival of nine nights fasting, praying, 'Garba' dancing musical extravaganza begins at month end to review all youth, elders & children to enjoy with new vigor & fashionable trends, involve re-vitalize all alike to unite with full might.

November: Autumns arrival, spring festival, fresh flowers, fruits, veg's, After Dussehra, Diwali, biggest festival of lights begins. Colorful dresses, Rangoli, flowers decorations reigns, crackers burst ban, regain thursts jubilation deals.

December: Winter chills sets in, Christmas jilts begin. Gliding, sliding reindeers' sledge, Santa's skates hedge, snowfalls flakes, Gifts galore, different varieties of candles, Chocolates, puddings, donuts & Cakes.

*****

18. 21st Century Analog

Mobiles, Laptops latest models, present trends

WWW.com. wider market trades blends

Malls, Hotels, Gyms appease

Oft' children demand please

Pasta, Pizza, Noodles Italian or Chinese

Fixed up office routine home chore

Relaxed body bliss minds adore.

Facebook, WhatsApp, You-Tube, Twitter, Instagram,

Social media, blogs, text messages slog jitters.

Swift fingers swell, thumb monitor atop

dwell
Recharge, Sim-cards, E-mails, all's well.
Online shopping, banking, debit-credit card
payment bills sell.
Improved version package claims
Selfies, Instagram, PUBG games
Few cheats too, cyber-crime blames,
New genre's high ambition aims.
So far so good- forward marching youths
brood.
Ms. Beautiful, Mr. Cool, developing nations
tool.
World's global warming dude, Isn't April
fool.

Dredges, sledges seasonal draught,
Realty boom, forests slot greenery fired rot.
Birds, animals, fishes breed extinct.
Sand mining, erosion's, fresh habitats
precinct.
GST- strides, high rates property stints,
Foresight de-monetize bids, new currency

mints.
Poor masses cloak, clip, clink, wise blink.

Public apathy- stretched utmost sympathy
Clod, clog, clout cloudburst cloudy.
Cleanliness drives, building toilets strives,
Re-join rivers, streams, annals-canals jives.
United we stand, divided we fall,
Balcony clappers drives droll.
Sunday evening torches lit,
Electricity, water supply resume bit by bit.

Captains, Copters help avoid brain drain,
Engineers shun flooding tracks by heavy
rains.
Tunnels dug waylaid metro, mono, bullet
trains.
Aadhar-Card protests, students' unrests,
Gullible ladies' day out, media mars,
Provoked religious lot Jam parks.

Hotchpotch, huddle hullaballoo bowel,

Hubbub hoydens hover out of hovel.
Incessant rains deluge delusions,
Miserable masses sick shuffle shovel.
Government bans noise pollution,
Fun-fair festive celebrations.

As quakes shake villages, towns,
Great leaders' demise, flags downed
Martyr blood spills, colorful wreaths
profound.

Heavy showers wipe off dark clouds' duster.
Choppy ravage mansions razed,
Fake news rumor, readers scared,
Lives' toll as diseases spread.
Medics beaten, strike uproars jolt,
Beware! Kins' react, ravage revolt,
Fraternity hitch-hike risky bolt.

Wise leaders decide to make air pure,
Lockdown of nations, safe & secure.
Gender bias, shrines closed, malls, theaters

shut.
Roads, Railways, Airways too stop their rut.
Schools' Colleges closed to protect kids
Since genocide rises, world over bids.
Pandemic, Pandemonium breaks,
Mobs moan at hospital gates.

Corona, Covid-19 stakes death rates,
Para-medics rescue with medical aids.
Flight passengers quarantined,
Society members in apartments bind,
Clumsy coerce dare,
Punitive Isolation despair.
Red, Orange, Green zones,
Institutes divided, restrict prone.

Essential goods Items only open,
Chemists' stores nearby residence with
drone token.
E-learn & E-perks project work,
'Home sweet home'-housewives luck.
Unemployed youth agitate as lives stuck jerk,

Literates demand education pattern change,
Backward masses favor skilled range.

Face-wash, Hand-wash sanitation,
Poor slots & slums fumigation,
Disinfectant smash viral splash.
Wicked quiz, 'How's the josh?'
'Clean neat tidy posh!'
Protection gears, masks, gloves pair,
Social distancing sequel, public senate blare.
Elephants, Tigers, Monkeys risk life jinx,
Human race plight survival tricks.

Scientists' prepare medical potion
Due Panacea, scanty ration.
Aftermath infernal attack tack,
Vaccination drive protect sycophant stac.
Convivial, convoke, convulse
Cook up recipe, bug-house blows.
Laughter challenges, pompous shows.

Evade, evaluate laymen, caste-creed code

rows.

Multiplex, motels blooms shaken
Wise, rigid step-by-step re-open.
No crowded local trains,
Gloomy lanes, Ambulance
Nay any street hawkers abound,
Police Vans guard all around.

Value of life glory rapped,
Nature's fury zip-zapped.
Extended lockdown, existence raise
Life begins anew with
Caution, care & praise.

*****

19. What is Life

Life is a challenge	Meet it
Life is a gift	Accept it
Life is an adventure	Invite it
Life is sorrow	Overcome it
Life is a tragedy	Face it
Life is a game	Play it
Life is a mystery	Unfold it
Life is a spirit	Release it
Life is a song	Sing it
Life is beauty	Praise it
Life is love	Enjoy it
Life is an opportunity	Take it
Life is a goal	Achieve it

Life is a struggle	Fight it
Life is a puzzle	Solve it
Life is a promise	Fulfill it
Life is a duty	Do it
Life is responsibility	Perform it
Life is a journey	Complete it

*****

20. Sour Eyes

Good days will come, bad days will fade

Better be prepared for the grind, God

forbade.
Awkward life's challenges do wade
When you get lemons, make lemonade.

Sometimes they have unique taste
Neither bother, nor make haste,
Just be smart to cut & paste,
The best out of waste.

Strict vigil on life-line,
Never cow down the mine
Mind your words, that's fine
Rest assured, you will shine.
Don't you worry
Meditate pray, let the asses bray
Every dog has its day.
Evils get punished, clumsy way
Evolve, revolve, world's a big 'O'
Friends & foes come-go.

New young bride's forehead spot glow
Owners delight, Neighbor's envy

Autumn, rainy, spring or snow.

Peeping toms, hiding domes
Creating freak mystic norms,
Alluding harsh glaring frowns,
Where from you come to flow?

Delinquently hoodwink to ply,
Upon the vast open dilate sky.
Rueful monotony, malign malice,
Supersede mighty bright ambience.

Pessimists fret & frown around,
Optimists crawl & brawl to maul,
Ironical subdue symphony call.
The new couples' altercations.

Regressive Genre gentry patience
Oblivious, autistic, deceit entities
Visualize sly, smirk intrepid deities.
Fortify ostracism gnawing ounce by ounce,
Every lethargic reckoner ever ready to

pounce.

*****

21. Nuts & Bolts

BA., B.Com., B. Sc.,

MA., M.Com., M.Sc.,

M.Ed., CA. CS., MBBS.,

BTech., MTech., FRCS.,

PISI; IG., DC., IPS., & IAS.,

Cracked up all to debase personal haughty haul.

Baneful, boastful baffle ball.
Tough stuff walnuts, daring to nail,
Hard rock pieces of beetle-nuts trial.
Fresh cashew-nuts toasted pale,
Grounded peanuts roasted well.
After wedding bliss suffice,
Newts, duets couples' surmise.

Become proud parents to flourish & rise
Rearing, caring new-born, profound wise.
Now the solid sordid part arises,
Of being good father/mother midst all novice.

Though beginnings always seem so nice
Dry almond nuts, Good-Day cookies mince.
Nourish to widen little hearts chestnuts.
Wheel of life-spokes encircle around,
You win some prize & loose abound.

Dealing all active, passive strife
Spiritual, ritual, mental, physical tiffs,
To mother/father a child's life.
Your body & mind turn domestically wild.
Bearing patience, tackling daily hassles,
Quench your thirst peg by peg,
All kinds of physical, mental agony turn
nutmeg.

Scold, hold, fold, risk, frisk bother
Then final loving title of dear father/mother
smother.
Throwing off shackles of golden chains,
Diamond rings, painful nose pins banes,
As carefree rising stature myths drain.

They then reckon to form family tree frame.
In their fields as children dabble,
Yearn, learn to collect small pebbles,
Become tough nuts, stubborn rock stone.
Parents churn in & out, rot, clot, bone by

bone.

Feigning Ignorance bliss, besides politely
You are pursued, followed quietly,
Since all prefer to stay free at random,
Enjoy a bit our new-found freedom.
Tapped to acquire traditional customs,
Deviate into societies systems.

Enriching the lovely family cocoon,
Far away from the weird world pollution,
You have to conclude a final solution.
When you realize fading gloom,
Descending order of the full moon,
You are not born with the silver spoon.
Guts & grit grip to prove your worth,
Potion by portion position out of cocoon,
Behold bold prudent prune business tycoon.

Been there, done that all with perfection,
Calm & cool dawns the maturation.
Daring life's sordid past, whichever creed or

caste,
No living/non-living matters ever last.

Existing for near & dear ones, you try to be busy,
Caught up in the new web of controversy,
Senior citizens help as you fall dizzy,
Spirits occult hold you to rise in fragrance breezy.

Ennoble trance efface, effete, efficacy.
Garnished food, posh status, designer valuables,
Egocentric, egress elaborates vicious life-cycle.
Hypocrite, hyperbole tests, convert hysteric debacle.
scrapped, broken parts mingle in dust shambles,
Purified by pure water & fire,
God particle, they all hire to admire.

*****

22. Budding Couple Bubbles

Although he is a cool guy
Minding his own business, doesn't pry.
Fond of dressing well prim, proper prisms
Trying hard for gentle mannerisms.
Favours to cook good food,
Lavish routine stubborn mood.

Surrounds himself with cheerful scents
Attar, Incense sticks varied perfume blends,
Change in behaviour nowadays prevails
Smoking, drinking tea often derails,
Tensed up feeling reflexes,
Grown up teen daughters' stress
Asking purpose of my life,
'Forever to be dutiful wife'.

Strange mettle, vague dealing
Recent motive, constant mocking,
Late night home returns, with fret & sweat,
Sorry for creating anxiety regret.
Unpaid rent, high electricity, grocery bills,
Prolonged school, college fees,
Abuse on trivial money hassles
Fumes, frets on silly matters.

Pointing fingers to one another
Avoid it, to be responsible rather.
Been there, done that arguments

Mental physical harassments.

One-upmanship male chauvinist

My sympathies, oh! Astrologist.

Toppling, faking, coping allowed,

Cheating not at all prowled.

Contoured seat in wedding bliss plight,

Never ever is a performance delight.

*****

23. Halloween

Oh! Gosh this Halloween affair

Get lost with your weird goggles pair

Why, you make me scare?

Hoodwink, hop off with your mare.

As I am a special breed rare,
Whom the socialites' care.
See how tiny drops perspire
Rouge ruse, rotten rout despair,
Such drastic stuff to hire,
Beware, of the consequences dire.

Nightmarish chill, dessert horror,
Creating fearful dare terror.
Don't frighten me, I'll hoot & wail
All in group, will surround with stones to
hail.
Come out of your hood,
Bring some dry wood
Tiny twigs, scattered sticks,
Gather all fallen leaves,
Help to light this archly autumn bonfire,
Strike off the gory darkness to retire.

Buck up! Stave off, else I'll steer,
Future genre of minds to bear,
To make the milieu clear

Make-up for the wear & tear.

*****

24. Let Sense Prevail

Ah! Shrewd shrug Engineer
Fix me up in the right gear.

I am ready for a trial,

Hurry up! So much to nail,

Pick up your steely shear,
Without any random fear.

Use any hard or software,
Wheel steady the pressure steer.

Dare to face fierce gory leers,
Give me appropriate attire.

Train to follow up this satire,
Internet, cyber-cafe avail,

Let the chip chisel
Choppy chord chivalry bane.

Din, dine, dip, dire dame
Nobody has to blame.

Nothings goanna dispel,
May good common sense prevail.

*****

25. Sharp Jitters

An absent-minded housewife,

Once lost her kitchen knife,

She searched for it thoroughly rife,

That jaded essential tool of daily strife.

On the dining table, under the gas,

Besides the sink & dustbin mess.
Passing by all possibilities, why couldn't she find?
Harrowing thoughts engulfed her mind,
Don't try to play with me hide & seek,
Else, will have to bear a rap rare kick,
To fall down from the Himalayan Peal Peak.
Or loose & break my molar teeth
Thinking of all such drastic briefs,
My heart started pounding heavy breath,
Why you make me to so much boil,
I'll shape your body in a coil,
Wrap & pack up in aluminum foil,
To deep fry in hot oil.
Or keep in freeze to solid cool,
Understood you bloody fool.
Such horrid hyper hype creeped,
As I lay in the noon nap bed pad peal & peeved,
In the evening opened the fridge,
Pulled out paper packets of veggies in a rage,
Gosh! Clink clinked out the favorite little

knife,

to my utter jolly moil, toil, mollify self,

Regained lost strength to climb up the cliff,

Picked up the ship-sharp martial support of my life,

Whacked off, all dark dingy dusts,

That clouded my mind with guile bursts.

*****

26. Tension

At the end of the dark dungeon tunnel

A small flick of light rebel,

Aftermath lockdown, Corona Covid spell,

God's temple lamp lit at home bright.

A solemn prayer, give little might.

To brave the health hazards,
& cast down climatic mars sight.
Back to pavilion, well treated patients,
Get well soon, Impious, envious notions.

Stern youth Icon dream Illusion myths,
Alone, aloof, cool, calm bliss stiffs.
No cat-fights, no dog-bites,
Neither rats run, nor lizards crawl, roaches' drawls.
Can't we read or write, by dim or dime,
Study without disturbing grime,
& hear true news sublime.
Students' hard work gone vain,
Undue travel prowl pain.
No exams declared, then delayed,
Far away boards, centers' ordained.
Monotony gone haywire,
Dominance development mire.

Mono, metro rail, Imported brand Tyre,

New elevators, flyover pyres.

Headaches, body aches, frustrating state,

We need a break, start anew afresh awake.

Let bygones, be gone inlet past,

Innovate peaceful means, let's adopt the best

Not detach & delude within creed or caste.

*****

27. Land of Peace

Can we expect,

a better prospect?

To live in this world compact,

with some dignity and respect.

In a Land of Peace, Land of Peace, Land of

Peace.
Mollify, regain, realm, reap,
Rear, recount, redeem, appease
Without disease, fear series,
Corona, Covid phases degrees,
In a Land of Peace, Land of Peace, Land of
Peace.

Praying for soulful release,
Meditate to cool off all malaise, freeze
Refresh, breathe pure air breeze,
Nobody could steal, push, pinch or squeeze.

In a Land of Peace, Land of Peace, Land of
Peace.
No strain, stress feel,
Walk with good interest & zeal,
Polite pleasing deal,
To procure a two square meal,
In a Land of Peace, Land of Peace, Land of
Peace.

*****

28. Friends chatter

All that matters

How are you?

Oh! Fine, Thank you

& what about you?

I am doing well

Pulling on, struggling to gel.

Why long time, no see?

Yeah! I was out of town, you see

Where have you been exactly?

My native place, Siliguri.

So that's why you look hale & hearty, healthy.

Phew! My marriage is fixed buddy,

So who is the lucky charm?

See my engagement snaps, be calm.

Wow! When is the D-day?

Next week on Sunday.

Help me, would you? Smart guy cue?

Why not? Don't you panic,

Just chill, chink

I will surely chum, let's pack & pick,

I don't know how to go about it.

Happens, as too much happiness comes to jostle, gist,

Come, we will make a to-do list.

Thanks, you are my best friend indeed.

What is your estimate budget?

Yes, I will let you, don't fret.

Okay Then, I will meet you tomorrow.

Let me know beforehand, if you want to borrow.

Yes, you guessed it right, that's my plight.

I will come, as always in foresight.

Bye, see you soon,

Take care, Good day Sonu, stay in tune,

Good luck for your honeymoon!

*****

29. Naturals

Nature oh! Nature, you give & take

In proportionate rate.

Vacant Isle’s rivers, mounts,

Flourish crops, flowers, fruits trees abound

Birds, animals, fishes varied species around.

You induct life in all
Input, Integrate knotty knoll.
Harmonious habitats horizon hone hue,
Horrid huddle hail due.

Ruby red, golden stretch, orange fresh anew
White, purple, pink lilies,
Blue, yellow morning glories blew.
Greenery regale reign, beauty queen,
Pride scenario prima prestige serene.
You impart seasonal rampart rap,
Through hot, cold, rainy jab in every sap.
Gentle, gentry genial gear up
Forbear, foresight, forsake sup.
Keeping the solar cycle balance induce,
Trot, tumult, tune, truce.

*****

30. Ways of life

My life is going on, on & on,
Through up's & downs from the time born.
Getting the experiences of life,
Sweet, sour & sharp like knife.

Studying, playing & enjoying,
Realizing dangers & also daring, praying.
For the fear of failure, working hard,

Hoping to get through to crawl ahead.

Trying to bring the strengthen might,
In the mind full of fright & fight.
Expecting for a few rays of light,
At the end of tunnel, that's gripping me tight.

Fixing aims, objectives for future,
Saddening a bit, at this juncture.
Being a girl, I am getting bored,
Nothing's in my hand, though adored.

*****

31. Happy Teacher's Day

Learning is the weightless treasure,

One can carry around easily forever.

Inner souls inspire to hire,

Eternal bliss, in oasis mire.

Enthrall, entail, enshroud,

To make the pupils proud.

Try to be a rainbow in someone's cloud,

As water is the driving force, nature applaud.

Since humility is essence of spiritual

knowledge,

We can share, care, bare all age.

Good advice is rarer than rubies,
Teachers can give to student buddies
Guidance to glide with pride,
Enrich aims to race, grace highest pole ride,
as to reach their goals far and wide.

32. Life's Innings "(in-ings)"

Late night studying, writing,
Drooping, dozing, snoring,
Waking up snarling, screeching, stretching,
Brushing, cleaning, bathing, wiping,
sneezing, freezing
Washing, clothing, Ironing, dressing,
Praying, break-fasting, revising, memorizing
Parents strictly send regular schooling.
Meeting neighbor aunty, uncles, wishing
good morning,
Reaching exam center hurrying, worrying,

Classmates, hi-bye best wishes sharing.

Some students lobbying, fooling,
Calling, stalling, pulling, copying,
troubling studious classmates, pranking,
Writing, racing to finish soon at proper
timing.
Teacher regularly supervising,
Catching hold of ruffians,slapping.

Out of class, dismissing for bullying,
Scolding, remarking, punishing, shaming,
Friends complain each other pointing.
Some cheating, copying murmuring
going on as, Miss's attention diverting.
Checking others talking, chatting, distracting,
Standing, Walking, moving than sitting,
Warning the class to pin-drop silencing.

Bell ringing warning! Finally, students stop
writing.
Collecting papers, scaling stamping, signing

Falling in line row-wise, quietly all
dispersing.

*****

33. Vacation Train Journey

Children enjoy holidays playing,
Cycling, skating, hiding-seeking,
Day dreaming, cloud forms observing,
Parents busy enlisting, booking,
To native place for holidays going,
Little anxiety happening,
Long train journey travelling,
Reserved sleeper bogeys searching,
Kids start humming, singing,
By window seat, hooraying.

Luggage, baggage on their hands & back,
Passengers greet each other, cordial task.
Enquiring, telling destinations as they ask,
Moving fast to get in soon to bask.
Slowly train starts excitement creating,
As speed picking up with loud siren horning.
Sun sets dark gloom spreading,
Lights put on, elders start praying.
Children fear to stare out, stop window gazing,
Glass shutters shut down closing.

Through dark tunnels & caves,
As the train speeds hollow hovel gales,
Counting them at stations pause paves,
Noting, pointing, jotting down milestone engraves.
TTE. Coming for tickets checking,
Extra load of boxes, parcels hanging, some hiding,
Seat exchanging, fine charging,

Rules abiding info sharing,
Tickets clipping & signing,
On a trunk by door side, TTE. Resting,
After duty in the corner adjusting.

Coupons distributed for dinner dining
Train stops at station, waiters running,
With food packets supplying, serving,
All passengers reliving, smiling, relishing,
Everybody tired want to lay down sleeping,
Suitable bed-sheets pillows arranging,
Main lights put off, fans speed regulating,
Dim lights lit, red alert chain seen clinging.

One & all lay over on upper berth climbing,
Center seat hooked up hanging,
Below seat all gently sleep swinging,
Without anybody hardly pushing.
Never can anyone sleep so cuddled up
slightly shaking,
In spite of station announcer's noises
annoying.

At dawn break some get up soon to be
afresh,
As occupied constantly, wash room's a busy
messy mess.
Day break's scenic rising sun's hue,
Everlasting bliss, blessings due, bright
sunrise view.
Morning commotion at stations
Stall vendors, waiters vie each other
promotion.

To compete with vertex verve, move further
Shouting, climbing, clinking harder
Supplying vials of water, cool-drinks, hot
tea-coffee, snacks,
Urging steely nerve barracks,
Such vibrancy & meadow views,
Cast away drowsy, dizzy eyes to subdue
tracks.

Constant fresh air vent ventilates free
venture

Vivacious mirth of adventure departure.
Brunch in shaking motion,
Noon siesta better potion.

Trains travels valuable notion,
Console, continuous, constrain feel,
Enhance, enrich in us new zeal
To mingle, jingle though single deal.
Besides mirage fear, bore tire,
Brave adverse dire mire,
Rise admire & desire
To quaff nature's bounty treasure.

*****

34. Visit site

At last after the long track trail
We get down at our native place Sangli frail
Coolies hurry up, shift baggage bale
Ranting, rating, pause, pale.
Our village kins welcome hail,
we relieve, refresh, inhale.
Grand parents clasp us to thrust
Moisten eyes hurts, gaiety gag burst,
Pure coconut water quenches our thirst,
As we race to drink & finish first.
Bigger rooms of home for relaxing,

Wide open lawns for playing,
Good food, new hoods, visiting, inviting,
All relatives' pleasantries, gifts exchanging.
Summer's heat, winter's cool, rainy drools,
Autumn's fresh colorful flowers blooms
Natives bask in nature's lovely propel pools.
Farming, planting, gardening,
Rearing, bearing, cattle grazing,
Gathering, giving, sharing, caring,
Coconuts, mangoes, paddy pairing,
Picking, counting, keeping, storing,
Dusting, cleaning, washing, fishing, swimming,
Peeling slicing veg's, cooking rice dumplings,
Mixing, fermenting, making delicacies tasting,
Heating, frying, baking puddings,
Delicious dishes relishing,
Joking, cracking, poking, laughing,
Fooling, Idling, pulling, plotting,
Calling, stalling, faking, tracking,
Shifting, staying, prying, planning,

Scaling, mountaineering, scarring,
Fearing, steering, daring, horrifying,
Trembling, grumbling, repelling, revolting,
Pack up day nearing, everybody parcels bringing,
Bags, sacks, packing,
For sendoff few coming,
With moist eyes elders hugging, kissing, blessing,
Cousins handshaking, sad feeling,
We get in the cab, luggage loading,
To the station driving, all good-bye hands waving.

*****

35. Struggling

Vacation ending, back to pavilion returning,
Matriculation passing, college joining,
Training, straining, whining, crying,
Battling, rattling, exams cracking,
Reading, writing, churning, groaning,
Struggling, wriggling, glorifying,
High grades scoring, gracing,
For achieving best results, medals winning,
Rankers, Toppers certificates collecting,
Get teacher's blessings, joyful back-patting,
Parents great reliefs deserving,
Job seeking, career planning,
Sky limits path showing, Youth glowing,
Arousing anxiety, consulting guidance

seeking,
Interviews nerve-wrecking,
No vacancy excuses releasing,
New start-up business following,
Policing, promotion, demotion, compelling,
Polling, voting, politicizing,
Selecting, electing, picking, choosing,
New car, home buying,
Now eligible for blissful wedding,
Hurrying, calling, ringing,
Texting, courting, gladdening,
Blushing, gushing, cocooning,
Life well settling, preserving,
Reserving, computing, risking, frisking,
Investing, Instituting, Industrializing,
Loans taking, debts mounting,
Bigger risks taking, scams scheming,
Loans defaulting, cheques dishonoring,
bouncing,
Calls ringing, creditors scolding, debtors
warning,
Assessing assets properties, case filing,

Naming, defaming, distressing, disgusting,
Advocates hiring, show-cause show casing,
Fretting, fuming, neglecting, calculating,
Wife harassing, scaling, wailing,
Glass breaking, stone pelting,
Rivals, bothering plotting, dislocating,
Family fearing, trembling, forgo outing,
Police protection guarding,
Smoking, drinking, work load increasing,
Late coming home, housewife angry
getting,
Stressing, straining, quarreling, fighting,
Trying hard adjusting, anxiety causing,
Sickness dampening,
Business agents, political parties supporting,
Communities help address changing,
Calm cool quiet town side areas selecting,
Settling down relaxing,
Glaring, blaring, reproducing,
Evil eyes avoiding, luxuries banning,
Shifting to middle class living,
Loving, caring, baby-sitting,

Arranging decent society living,
Wife nagging better life style standard deserving,
Married life horrifying, clashing,
Wife-beating, demanding divorcing,
Mending, bending, forwarding,
Belting, melting, Icing,
When kids' mischief mongering,
Cycling, skating, running, exercising,
Falling down knee hurting,
Washing, cleaning, medicine applying,
Buying, toying, kids' kidding,
Demand fashionable dressings folding, molding,
Changing life styles mounding,
Harrowing, narrowing, sorrowing,
Headache, body ache, fever coming, going,
Steaming, massaging, better feeling,
Get well soon cards, friends sending,
Forgetting, forgiving, rivalry fading,
Tempers rising, global warming,
Hurly-burly seasonal changes surprising,

Torpid, torrent, tornado tormenting,
Treacherous trivial treason's tremors
trouncing,
Aged grandparents & parents falling sick,
dying,
Grim grip, grisly growl grueling,
Hyper hype hypocrisy, hysteria hurting,
Deranged derelict derail depriving,
Insane desires desist, despair deriding,
Destiny despise bitter defaming,
Deflate defy, delete delicate parting,
Leaving abroad for better prospects
extending,
Webbing, networking, profits gaining,
Non-Residents' status uploading,
Smart home searching,
Renting, rating, budgeting,
Society sniffing, details investigating,
Some lewd remarks passing, criticizing,
Holding back day to day routine
proceedings,
Blocking, catching in lift by stopping,
Electricity switch off putting,

Initial hick-ups, we don't mind caring,
Silly matters, avoid arguing,
Our concise concrete concord reconciling,
Envious stares neglecting,
Though clogged coarse cluster coercion's pulling,
Water supply starting with watchman whistling,
Families store water, suitably using,
Value of time, water, electricity gradually all learning,
Wife, children mocking, joking,
Miser, stingy fringy remarks passing,
Braving, saving, borrowing, balancing,
Debtors, creditors, predators prying,
So, simple sample living,
Ignorance fuming, example setting,
For children & society following,
At night children crying, mosquito biting,
Mummy sleeping tired, tummy turmoil's, legs swelling,
Daddy wakes up provide nettings,

Next day morning, newspaper reading,
Attends society meetings, complains accepting,
Advising municipal intervention, In-charge obliging,
Area surroundings sweeping,
Drainage cleaning, fumigating,
Festivals approaching, children enjoying,
Hopping, Jumping, dancing, swinging,
After grateful home-coming,
Teaching, preaching, socializing,
Troubling problems Listening,
Understanding trying solving,
Gaining faith society recognizing,
Bold daring plights challenging,
Middle class status promoting,
Elders gracefully adhere meditating,
Friends helping, family cooperating,
All's well that ends well stating,
Oh God! So much fervent imbroglio impelling,
Whew! Enough of all blatant positioning,

Recovering, regaining, Re-incarnating,
Afresh into gifted super natural beings.

36. Farm House

Nature teacher, tree preacher,
protects from predators,
Parapet walls, creepers atop,
shady shadows abrade.
Hot sunny noon ablaze
As the farmers raze
Wild long grasses & weeds
Plucked off to sow new seeds
Of varied fruits, flowers yield
Crops & veg's hybrid.
The myriad milieu merge, urge,
Mysterious mire surge.
Watering along drupel divergent drizzle
Dredge dregs drench,

Drill, droll, droop on the ranch.
Small sprouts wriggle out,
From sediment sedge seep snout.
Sun’s rays seize the sepal sap,
Set, fret, frisk with vigorous tap,
To open up, grow fast its tab.
The pebbles path to tag.
Flog, Corn, rice flakes flail,
Underneath the snails’ hail,
Germs to germinate well.
Gardener sprays germicides,
Tends garden fruits, flowers trails,
Spiders’ spin webs to trap flies, gnat banes.
Parse views, bushes, shrubs, reeds,
Chivalry chord choral chore freed,
Orchids, carnations, chrysanthemums
bounty breed.
Bees, dragon flies buzz, pollen pods heed,
Caterpillars cater to cedar cede,
Carnal style cocoons guild.
Butterflies fly, daffodils dahlia lure,
Beehives heap hung horde spare pure,

Warbler warbles wanderlust dare,
Hither-thither everywhere.
Wagers swagger grab straws wag,
Paddy sacks, sag, zigzag,
Thatch, thrust gab gabble adjust,
Perky pesky pests burst,
Wane kids wallow wanton vaunt,
Guffaw, gamut, game of marbles count,
Nag, prescient mess, nestling nest
Put in grain crumbs crust
Crows caw-caw, cuckoos coo, shoo them off,
Scamp silly brats, scare jump scoff.
Gibe giggle gesture,
Gobble cassava lumps, pastime pasture.
Mango mellows, melon chunks,
melody medley bellows billows puns.
Bovines graze cud chew moo,
Juicy green grass laden with dew.
Cowboy ties necktie jingle,
Sheaf, turf, tug, shuffles,
Milking coy calf push, pull belly nipples.

Rams rambles, goat's hotchpotch tremble,
Quench their thirst, by trees shades yonder.
Pigs grunt, in porch poultry clucks, ducks' quacks together,
Horses neigh, foals ponder on the fodder,
Kennel hounds' barks, puppies' mew, cats purr louder,
Squirrels', rabbits, gophers, squeak
Peep through their hollow burrows peak.
Mynahs, sparrows, pigeons peck-pluck grains heap.
Hens' pell-mell, chicks cackle, ducks revel,
Kites Egrets Eagles hover high, prey, glide marvel,
Parrots, petrels, doves peep-pop jaunt jay,
Swine's' oinks moil-toil muddy germs, worms away,
As piglets sway gay.
The flora fauna emanates,
Fragrance emerges permanent,
Evoke, exert grace great.
Granary granulate, grandeur grange,

Gratifying, gratitude wide range.

*****

37. Diwali

Festival of lights, sparkling bright
Decor tunes twinkle every sight
Throughout dark cool nights
Spreading joys to ban scare & dare.

Old rags scraps sold off rot
New comforts, luxuries bought
Clean houses, whitewashed paints
Greetings, meetings, for new year gains.

Share markets rise-fall trends
Puja rituals of accounts books main
Goddess of wealth Laxmi domain
Early morning ‘ubtan’ scent bath past.

New dress wears to look smart,
Feast first fast, sweets snacks part.
Colorful Rangoli designs packs cheer heart
Sand powders, flowers all around mart.

Small mud clay oil lamps surround,
Every homes' entrance doors windows abound.
Dry fruits sweetmeats treat,
Throngs shops, varied lanterns hanging fleets.

Courtesy exchange of sweets plates,
Gala galaxy of great dates.
Nick-knack knell,
Knock knoll know-how gel.
Grabs galore laughter gag,
Gaiety gale gamble tumble gab, fag.

*****

38. Y- Why

Mom: Why do you cry, my blue eyed Slovene sly?

Chubby kid: Can't I cry, why? No school, no outdoor play, No snacks, fruits display, Should I laugh, come-on try.

Pop: What do you desire? come with me, I'll buy. Corona, restrictions comply.Don't be so coy- doy, my cute boy.Wear your mask, be ready to ply.

Chubby kid: I don't want new dress, But new mobile, for online study & gaming joy.

Mom: So that you sit with it whole day & don't listen or obey what I say, To become stubborn nutty fray.

Chubby kid: Then should I just fret, fume, foray.

Pop: And strain your eyes, with fingers disarray.

Chubby kid: Oh! So disgusting gloomy dismay.

Pop:Well, we need a hair-cut, come let's move away.

Chubby kid: I am coming only if you heed my way.

Pop: Okay chum, promise me you will be sane, Don't overload your brain, Be smart helpful to your mom again, I' ll surely get the mobile you claim.

Chubby kid:Wow! Thankyou pop, mom, my precious gem

Mom: C'mon don't praise us so much to exclaim, We know you are our lucky fame.

*****

39. Children's Day Mothers Pray

Little angels sent by God,
Messenger of peace bonding pod,
Post-natal potent pot,
Potter pouting to pounce not.
Praise braze bravura bare,
Mom tom's pomp bizarre dare,
After topsy-turvy topple tornado fare.
A slight glee glance of Newt's care,
The first mew cry of tiny tot's snare.
Snarl snatch to be born again without scare.
Though scarce scar scamper in the rear.
As new Sunrise shine raze,

Readmit, rebind faith haze.
Reap, realm dazzle daze,
Deaf deal with dear dawn dawdles,
Debunk all relations claims in cradle,
To rock-a-by baby with sweet lullaby babbles.
Struggling to hastily haggle,
Past destiny's misfortune hassles.
Hush! Push, bedtime stories rush,
Daydreams of her growing kid gush.
Feeding, breeding, considering,
Wealth of health regaining,
No more follies, pitfalls vows,
caution nurse soft dolls paws.
As the bundle of joy toddler utters,
Umm…Aaa…Pa…Pa…Mum…mum mutters',
Cute lilt voices, sparkling wide eyes,
Arouse moms to rise,
Move about shedding all load of bonded guise.
Thanks god for no handicaps,
In the offspring's body or scalp.

Holding tight Ma's fingers,
Trying the first few steps lingers.
After slither, crawls, tumble jumble,
To guard safe every fall & drops crumble,
Put in the walker, buck up forward
With props & toys ahead powered.
The cute smile of joy, happiness,
Infatuate kid's parents dense.
As the breast- fed baby,
Spoils bed-wetting shabby,
Cleans, bathes change diapers grabby,
All day-night whacky, shaky, lackey.
Solid food cereals', packs,
Timely monitored diet hacks,
Medicines & vaccines tracks.
Biscuits, lollypop candies, chocolates,
Seasonal fruits, delicacy snacks.
First birthday celebration, great pomp show,
Balloons decors, Party cakes crispy wafers,
Gifts, cool drinks flow,
Kids enjoy merriment row
Parents rejoice, visit temples to bow,

Pray for long success in life to follow.
Play school, nursery, garden fleets,
Mommies proudly blabber in event meets.
Stubborn scatter of toys, books, food treats,
Ever gather replace, maintain good hygiene.
Bicycle bystander spectator squirt,
Beware of doggy's dogged spurt.
Back sprains bearing, injuries dressing,
Sportive sports speck spark gleaming,
Laundry washing solo scary jig,
Oh God! Such sordid rib tickling rip, rap,
rig.

*****

40. Baby Boon

Deemed apple of our eyes sparkle charm,
We deify deity of our orchid farm.
Infallible mettle delegate dam,
Soothing deign, soft palms jam,
Oh dear! You are such a precious gem.
Calm cool bliss relief balm,
In this messy metropolis dome mayhem.
Progeny prophecy prowess claim,
Rebuked rebel recants, pseudo malice maim.
Receded to punch pun punitive braze,
Exert, explore, extend solace.
Triumph vibrate yearn-pine phase,
Pinnacle pioneer, pious sublime grace.

*****

41. Nursery zest zenith

One, two, mobile, laptops brew,
Three, four open windows,
Five, six check- up E-Mail messages,
Password names,

Seven, eight, respond scroll Google, games,
Facebook, Instagram fames.
Nine, Ten bull’s eye gain, pain,

Pitter-patter rain storms drain.
Eleven, Twelve, deluge drench,
Disease pandemic vain.

Thirteen, fourteen, Oranges, lemons worth
sanity regain,
Fifteen, sixteen, lockdown, quarantine

zones strain,
Seventeen, eighteen, harmless vaccine
invention bargain.
Nineteen, Twenty, clean environs ensue,
enrich, domain.

*****

42. Jack & Jill

Ragged, ruined, split, deplete,
Went up the mount peak, tell-tale fleet.
Packed appeal with new zeal,

Skill shield flit,
Devour, devout, deuce, detour grit
Sack, sick, track, trick, brit bit.

For a pail of water dredge, dig, deal drench drill,
Droll, drone, drool, droop, dross to fill,
Buck up! Stack up c'mon Jack & Jill,

Spurt, Squirt, sprain knee, knell, kneel,
To skim brim as team esteem steam,
Haughty-Potty, potent portal milestone

realm ream.
No more falling down, tumble-fumble,
breaking crown,
Refresh, refrain, regain health forgone.

*****

43. Alphabets Order cord

A B C D E F G

Birds, rivers, breeze wander free,

Nobody scares in daydream bury.

I J K L M N O P

Relieve, release from wild gory ferry,

To be in hush- bush quiet gentry.

Q R S T U V W

See how high, sky is blue.

X Y Z

Have good food, go to bed,

Praise the Lord's glory with roses red.

*****

44. Literary Groups club

All the literates they say,
Can make a better world to stay,
Build strong base to lay,
Anybody could follow up, if they may,
Think it fit, to cross the bay.

As it isn't just the rhyming jingles
But great valour of strange minds mingles,
Of right thinking, perfect sense,
Direct script to balance,
Solemnify oneself onset onus talents.

Opine our views, without any offence,
Regard, respect everybody's preference
To earn, gain invaluable knowledge.
Unique, discreet to all sects ages,

In whichever forms of language pages.
Book lovers, readers, writers bask
Manifold vast fields unmask,
Natural artful unravel task.

*****

45. Bank

Eager, vigour spasms,
The rows of queue
Wait outside to pursue
Their hard- earned savings due
To safeguard secure amounts few.

Some Pass the buck, pray for luck,
Go for errands running amok,
Afterwards return back to tuck,
As they open the shutter & glass door,
Visitors enter one by one to pick-pluck,
adore.

Account holders move in & out,
Complete formalities, quick on the spot.
Varied mobile tunes, no frets or fumes,

Swift laptops, compute click-clock looms.
Past lunch time work assumes.
Stern, gentle guard ever alert,
Takes in requests ('KYC'), abrupt,
As elders wait patiently to spurt,
Seated on the couch, quite perturb
Till the officer's calls burst.

*****

46. Question and Answer

Who am I? Am I True?

Why me? Why not you?

What is the benefit? Is it fit?

What's the commotion?

Which caste, creed, nation?

Do they have any other notion?

When can we expect?

How do they propel their prospect?

Would you count?

Are you sure we can proceed?

Check- up the I-card

Aadhaar, Pan, Voter-Id

Oh! Sure, that's perfect.

Now can we live in peace?

After vaccination drive cease.

What nuisance, you believe?
Behave well, why so knave?
Can we live here without being so?
Don't be so gruff, bro,
But its gruesome, grudge tough,
All grooms grill & grind to ground.
Shed your niggard nick nimble bound,
Dumb, hermit to hinder around.
Then how should one be,
Like the twinkle little star,
High above the sky so far,
In darkness surround ajar,
Spreading its light to shine,
One can only dream, to be mine.

*****

ACKNOWLEDGEMENTS

Reserve, preserve, patience pays,
Don't be restless, reap gems in delayed ways.
Where there's a will, there's a way,
Even in darkness, recourse proves worthwhile.
Through hardship and regret, I found my voice,
Vented anguish into poetry, a versatile choice.
Dedications to loved ones, who anchored me,
Saved my journey, and helped me to be free.
Thanks to neighbors, friends, teachers, and guides,
Their advice and wisdom helped me to step inside.
Inspired, I nullified my fears, and found my way,
Grateful for contributions, and loved ones each day.

- Savita S. Dharan -

Email: arclinesliterary@gmail.com

www.ingramcontent.com/pod-product-compliance
Ingram Content Group UK Ltd.
Pitfield, Milton Keynes, MK11 3LW, UK
UKHW021340190726
13845UKWH00027B/652

9 789334 266603